A FAMILY IS FOREVER

Author's dedication:
To Grandmas and Grandpas everywhere—especially my
own grandparents,
Griffith John and Rosamund Eurgain Owen,
and
Joseph Haydn and Alice Evelyn Pritchard.

And my children's grandparents,
Gerald Edgar and Betty Lou Bessey
and
Noel Lewis and Patricia Ann Owen.

Artist's dedication:
To my Dad, Greg,
who always looks for an opportunity to teach.

Cover design copyrighted 2003 by Covenant Communications, Inc.

Published by Covenant Communications, Inc.
American Fork, Utah

Text copyright © 2003 by Siân Ann Bessey
Illustrations copyright © 2003 by Ben Sowards
Printed in China
First Printing: August 2003

15 14 13   10 9 8 7 6 5 4 3

ISBN 1-57734-879-6

A FAMILY IS FOREVER

WRITTEN BY
SIAN ANN BESSEY

ILLUSTRATED BY
BEN SOWARDS

Andrew loved visiting his grandma and grandpa. They lived down a long, graveled lane, in an old farmhouse surrounded by fields and trees.

On rainy days, muddy puddles dotted the lane. Andrew liked to put on a raincoat and rubber boots, and with Grandma's big, black umbrella above his head, he'd splash and splash and splash. Sometimes Grandpa made newspaper boats. Andrew sailed them in the biggest puddle— until they became too soggy to float.

When the warm sun shone, Andrew spent hours in a treehouse Grandpa had built among the branches of an oak tree. But the moment he smelled Grandma's homemade bread or cinnamony, sweet apple pie, he'd hurry down from his lofty perch.

Grandma baked all kinds of treats. Andrew's absolute favorite was her chocolate cake. On chocolate cake days, Andrew was Grandma's special helper in the kitchen. He'd sit on a tall stool with a big, white apron tied around his neck. As Grandma put the butter, sugar, eggs, and flour into the old blue bowl, they'd sing, "*When we're helping, we're happy*," and Andrew would stir all the ingredients together with a long, wooden spoon.

After Grandma poured the batter into a pan, she'd let Andrew scrape the bowl and lick the spoon. He often wondered why Grandma bothered baking the cake. It tasted so yummy right out of the bowl.

While he waited for dinner, Andrew liked climbing the staircase inside the house. Stair number three and stair number nine creaked. He'd always step over them on the way up, but on the way down he'd stop and purposely wiggle his feet—just to hear the wood squeak.

Tucked into one corner of a bedroom upstairs was a little feather bed. This was Andrew's bed whenever he stayed overnight. It was soft and warm. Andrew loved to burrow down under the covers and curl up like a squirrel in a hollow tree. He usually fell asleep right away. But if he lay awake, he'd stare at a photograph of an old man on the wall beside his bed.

It was the only thing at Grandma and Grandpa's house that Andrew didn't like. The picture was black, gray, and white—no colors at all. The man wore a dark suit. His gray hair was slicked back and his face, which was partly covered by a beard, was stern.

Although the photograph was fading, the man's eyes were bright and clear. To Andrew it seemed that no matter when he peeked out from beneath the bed covers, the old man was always watching him.

One summer night, after he and Grandpa had knelt together for prayers, Andrew crawled into bed and pulled the quilt over his head.

"What are you doing, Andrew?" Grandpa asked.

"Hiding," Andrew replied, his voice muffled by the bedclothes.

"Oh no," Grandpa chuckled, "no more hide-and-seek until tomorrow, young man."

"I'm not playing hide 'n' seek," came Andrew's muffled voice again. "I'm just hiding."

"Why are you hiding?" Grandpa asked.

"Because I don't want the scary man looking at me," Andrew said.

Grandpa sat down on the edge of Andrew's bed. "What scary man?"

Andrew pulled down the quilt until his eyes were uncovered. "That one," he said, pointing to the framed picture on the wall.

Grandpa's gaze followed the direction of Andrew's finger. Then he lifted his grandson onto his knee.

"Don't you know who that is, Andrew?" Grandpa asked.

Andrew shook his head.

"That's a photograph of my grandfather—Grandpa Humphreys."

"Your grandpa?" Andrew said. "But you're too old to have a grandpa."

Grandpa smiled. "Everyone has a grandpa, Andrew. Even old people like me. But people my age aren't able to see their grandparents the way you can."

"Because they're dead?" whispered Andrew.

Grandpa nodded. "Grandpa Humphreys lived in this very house. He was a farmer and worked hard all his life. Eventually he grew old. His body became tired and he died. His spirit left his body and went to live with Heavenly Father. He's there now, with family and friends."

"But if he's your grandpa, why does he look so mean?" Andrew asked.

"Oh, he wasn't mean," Grandpa said. "In those days it took so long to take a photograph, folks became tired of waiting with a smile on their faces, so they looked serious instead. But you know what I think . . . ?" Grandpa leaned forward and whispered into Andrew's ear. "I think he was wishing he could change out of his Sunday-best and go fishing instead."

Andrew studied the picture from the safety of his grandfather's arms. "D'you miss him?" he asked.

"Very much," Grandpa said. "He was the best grandpa anyone could have."

Andrew's head popped up immediately. "Not better than you!"

Grandpa smiled. "Well, I don't know. Grandpa Humphreys and I used to do all sorts of things together. In fact, I was about your age when he first took me to his favorite fishing hole—and we came home with the biggest fish you've ever seen."

Andrew eyes grew large and he squirmed upright on Grandpa's lap. "Could we do that too?" he asked.

Grandpa looked out the window at the rosy glow of the setting sun. "Looks like it's going to be a nice day tomorrow," he said. "Should be just about right for a fishing trip."

"Yeah!" Andrew clapped his hands. "To the special place with the huge fish?" he asked.

Grandpa tousled Andrew's hair with his calloused hand. "To Grandpa Humphreys's favorite fishing hole," he agreed. Then he lifted Andrew off his knee and placed him back under the bedcovers. "But first," he said, "sleep."

They set out the next morning. Grandma waved them off from the kitchen door. Grandpa carried two fishing poles and a tackle box. Andrew carried a brown paper sack with two ham sandwiches, two apples, and four of Grandma's chocolate-chip cookies inside.

The sky above was blue and the sun shone brightly. Grandpa led the way down the lane, past green fields full of cows and sheep. He whistled softly as they walked, pausing to admire a speckled brown feather and a very fat, hairy caterpillar that Andrew gathered along the way.

It wasn't long before they reached a wooden gate. Grandpa fiddled with the latch and it swung open on creaky hinges. Andrew waited until he'd closed it again before climbing up and over the sturdy slats.

He slipped his small hand into Grandpa's as they passed the grazing cattle. Some of the cows stopped to watch them. One lumbered closer, eyeing the lunch sack with interest. Grandpa saw the cow coming and called out to her. The cow stood still, twitching her ears, and blowing nervously through her nose. At last, she turned around and ambled back toward the herd.

Andrew breathed a sigh of relief and squeezed Grandpa's hand a little tighter—awfully glad he was there.

They cut through the trees at the far end of the meadow. All at once Andrew heard the merry sound of running water. Eagerly, he tugged Grandpa forward.

"I hear the river," he cried. "Are we almost there?"

"Almost," said Grandpa. He walked toward a cluster of large boulders at the water's edge. "Hmm," he said, eyeing the rocks carefully. "If I remember right, this one was Grandpa Humphreys's seat." He pointed to a medium-sized boulder, smoothed by the elements into a polished stool. "And that one next to it was mine."

Andrew walked up to the slightly larger boulder and ran his hand over its surface. He noticed the indentation near the top—a perfect place for a boy to sit.

"Grandpa," Andrew hesitated. "D'you think that since you're the grandpa now, and I'm the boy, that maybe you could sit on Grandpa Humphreys's rock and I could sit on yours?"

"I think that's a fine idea," Grandpa said.

Andrew watched while Grandpa cast the fishing line. It sang through the air, until the baited hook entered the river with a plop. Carefully, Grandpa reeled in the line and offered the rod to Andrew.

"Now you try," he said.

With his grandfather's hands carefully guiding him, Andrew cast the line out again. The reel whirred as the line spun free. Then came a second plop.

"Well done, Andrew," Grandpa said. "Grandpa Humphreys would be proud. The first time I tried doing that, my hook got all tangled up in the weeds."

Andrew's eyes sparkled. He sat on his rock, holding the rod tightly as Grandpa cast another line.

"Now then," Grandpa said. "How about some of that lunch Grandma gave us?"

Andrew nibbled a cookie. He watched the water rush downstream. It spouted over protruding rocks, swirled around a fallen tree limb, and rippled through the reeds at the river's edge. The only sounds were the distant lowing of cattle and the buzzing of busy insects in the nearby clover.

"Grandpa," Andrew said. "Did you really get your hook stuck in the weeds?"

"Yes, indeed," Grandpa said. "Poor Grandpa Humphreys waded out into the river up to his knees to untangle the line. But he didn't give up on me. By the end of the afternoon his clothes were dry and I could cast a fishing line all by myself."

"Did you catch a fish?" Andrew asked.

"I believe I did. We came here many times. Some days we returned home empty-handed, but every once in a while we'd catch enough fish to feed the whole family."

"Was I there then?" Andrew asked, wrinkling up his forehead trying to remember.

Smiling, Grandpa shook his head. "No, that was long before you were born. Your mother wasn't even born."

Did you have a different family?" Andrew asked.

"Oh, no," Grandpa said. "I'll always have the same family—and so will you. But we're not all on earth at the same time. When I was young, Grandma and Grandpa Humphreys were here, along with my parents and my two sisters. You, your mother, and your father were still with Heavenly Father, waiting to join us.

"I'm an old man now. My grandparents, parents, and sisters have all finished their lives on earth. They've gone back to live with Heavenly Father. I miss them, but your grandma, your parents, and you have joined me here—so I haven't been lonely."

"Are you going to go live with Heavenly Father too?" Andrew said, with growing concern.

Grandpa rose and put his arms around Andrew. "Someday I'll die—we all will, eventually. But when that happens, remember that we'll only be apart for a short time. Our family has been sealed in the temple, and no matter where I am, I'll always be your grandpa."

"Just like you and Grandpa Humphreys?" Andrew asked.

"Just like me and Grandpa Humphreys," Grandpa echoed, "because a family is forever."

Suddenly the rod lying across Andrew's knee jerked.

"Grandpa!" Andrew gasped.

"Hold it steady, Andrew. Hold it steady." Grandpa's hands covered Andrew's on the rod, and together they wound in the line.

Before long, Andrew heard wild splashing at the river bank. Seconds later the fish was out of the water and inside Grandpa's net.

Grandpa held up the net and gave a whistle. "I think you've inherited Grandpa Humphreys's gift for fishing," he said. "It's a beauty."

Andrew gazed at the shimmering fish. "Is it even bigger than the one you caught when you were little?" he asked.

Grandpa laughed. "Could be," he said. "It very well could be."

There were three fish in Grandpa's fishing basket when the two fishermen headed back to the old farmhouse. Andrew barely noticed the cows in the pasture, and didn't stop to pick up a single treasure along the way. He held his grandfather's hand until they came within sight of the house—then he started to run.

"Grandma!" he called, and when his grandmother appeared at the kitchen door, Andrew ran into her waiting arms. "We caught the biggest fish you've ever seen," he cried joyfully. "Come and see." Andrew helped Grandma cook fish for dinner that night. And it was a very tired but happy little boy who crawled into bed later that evening.

Once again, Andrew felt the gaze of Grandpa Humphreys from the photograph on the wall. Somehow it didn't bother him anymore.

"Grandpa showed me your special fishing hole today," Andrew said. "He caught a huge fish there, and I caught an even bigger one. It was the best day ever . . .

Andrew yawned. He snuggled down into the soft embrace of the feather bed. Looking back at the familiar portrait, he felt a soothing peace.

"When we see you again, we'll tell you all about it," he whispered sleepily.

Perhaps it was only a flickering shadow from the curtains swaying in the moonlight, but for an instant, it seemed to Andrew that Grandpa Humphreys's solemn eyes twinkled.